W9-ATQ-975

BRUMBACK LIBRARY
The parable of the sower /
Caswell, Helen Rayburn.   226.8 CAS
JNF   c1

3 3045 00026 2176

921016 $10.95
j226.8   Caswell, Helen
CAS   Rayburn.
                 The parable of
            the sower

CHILDREN'S DEPARTMENT
THE BRUMBACK LIBRARY
OF VAN WERT COUNTY
VAN WERT, OHIO

Parable of the Sower

WRITTEN AND ILLUSTRATED BY
Helen Caswell

Abingdon Press
Nashville

Abingdon Press
Nashville

Copyright © 1991 by Abingdon Press

All Rights Reserved.

Library of Congress Cataloging-in-Publication Data

Caswell, Helen Rayburn.
  The parable of the sower / Helen Caswell.
    p. cm.
  Summary: Recounts the New Testament parable that teaches readers
how to listen, and not just hear.
  ISBN 0-687-30020-7 (alk. paper)
  1. Sower (Parable)—Juvenile literature. 2. Bible stories:
English—N.T. Gospels. [1. Sower (Parable) 2. Parables. 3. Bible
stories—N.T.] I. Title.
BS378.S7C75 1991
226.8'09505—dc20
                                                   90-23200

PRINTED IN SINGAPORE

Parables are stories that have a hidden meaning.
You need to really listen to a parable
to find the hidden meaning.

Jesus told many parable stories. This one is called
the parable of the sower. Listen carefully, and see if
you can find the hidden meaning.

Once long ago, a farmer went out to sow seed in his field. It was a very large field, and it would have taken too long to plant each seed, the way we plant peas or beans in our gardens, so he carried the seed in a bag. As he walked very slowly along the path, he would reach into the bag, take out a handful of seed and, with a big sweep of his arm, throw the seed onto the ground.

Not all the seeds landed where they were supposed to. Some fell on the path, which was tramped down so solid and smooth that the seeds couldn't get into the soil at all.

Birds were flying along behind the farmer, hoping to eat some of the seeds, and they flew down right away and ate all the seeds that fell on the path.

Some of the seeds fell on places where there was only a thin layer of dirt over a big rock. Here the seeds sprouted quickly and sent up tall stems, but they couldn't send down roots because of the rock. So when the hot sun shone down on the plants, they wilted and died.

Some seeds fell in a patch of weeds that grew at one end of the field, and when the new little plants came up, the weeds crowded them out.

But most of the seeds fell on good soil, where they put down roots and sprouted and grew into big healthy plants.

When harvest time came, there was a fine big crop.

Jesus told this story to people a long time ago, and when he had finished, he said to them, "He who has ears to hear, let him hear." The story shows us the different ways people *listen*.

The farmer who sowed the seed was like someone
who tells people about God. Not everyone that person
talks to really *listens*.

Some people are so full of themselves that they never really listen to anything. They think they know everything already. These people are like the path that was so hard that the seeds couldn't get into the soil, and the birds came down and ate them.

Some people are like the thin soil over the rock, where the seeds couldn't put down roots. Those people may be all excited when they first hear the word of God, but they don't listen carefully, so they don't realize that they need to *do* something.

The seeds that fell among the weeds are like people who are trying to listen to too many things at the same time—they don't really *hear* anything.

But most people are like the seeds that fell on the good soil and grew up big and strong. When they hear the stories Jesus told, they really listen, because they know that hearing God's word is more important than anything else.